GW00759064

COUNTRY HOTELS

LANDHOTELS
HOTELS À LA CAMPAGNE
LANDELIJKE HOTELS

Edited by Macarena San Martín

Art director:
Mireia Casanovas Soley

Editorial coordination:
Simone Schleifer

Project coordination:
Macarena San Martín

Texts:
Macarena San Martín

Layout:
Francisco J. Castillo Moreno

Translations coordination: Equipo de Edición, Barcelona
Translations: Heike Reissig, Bonalingua Übersetzungen (German), Rachel Burden (English), Anne
Dumail (French), Fennie Steenhuis, Persklaar (Dutch)

Editorial project:
2008 © LOFT Publications | Via Laietana, 32, 4.°, Of. 92 | 08003 Barcelona, Spain
Tel.: +34 932 688 088 Fax: +34 932 687 073 | loft@loftpublications.com | www.loftpublications.com

ISBN 978-84-96936-26-3   Printed in China

Cover photo: © Pere Planells
Back cover photo: © Manolo Yllera

LOFT affirms that it possesses all the necessary rights for the publication of this material and has duly paid all royalties
related to the authors' and photographers' rights. LOFT also affirms that it has violated no property rights and has
respected common law, all authors' rights and other rights that could be relevant. Finally, LOFT affirms that this book
contains no obscene nor slanderous material.

The total or partial reproduction of this book without the authorization of the publishers violates the two rights reserved;
any use must be requested in advance.

If you would like to propose works to include in our upcoming books, please email us at loft@loftpublications.com.

In some cases it has been impossible to locate copyright owners of the images published in this book. Please contact the
publisher if you are the copyright owner of any of the images published here.

COUNTRY HOTELS

LANDHOTELS
HOTELS À LA CAMPAGNE
LANDELIJKE HOTELS

Edited by Macarena San Martín

„Die wahre Entdeckungsreise besteht nicht darin, neue Landschaften zu suchen, sondern mit neuen Augen zu sehen."

Marcel Proust, französischer Schriftsteller

"The real voyage of discovery consists not in seeking new landscapes but in having new eyes."

Marcel Proust, French novelist and author

« Le véritable voyage de découverte ne consiste pas à chercher de nouveaux paysages mais à avoir de nouveaux yeux. »

Marcel Proust, écrivain français

"De echte ontdekkingsreis bestaat er niet uit nieuwe landschappen te ontdekken, maar de dingen met andere ogen te bekijken."

Marcel Proust, Franse schrijver

12   SALOME'S GARDEN
Tom Green, Nigel V. Brown

20   TIGMI
Max Lawrence

30   DINAROBIN HOTEL
Maurice Giraud

38   CHAPWANI PRIVATE ISLAND
Maura Antonietto, Nigel V. Brown

44   RIAD ZINA MARRAKECH
Max Lawrence

54   LAKE MANYARA TREE LODGE
Chris Browne

252   HOTEL VILLA FIESOLE
Bianchini

SALOME'S GARDEN

The Last of the Royal Houses of Zanzibar

Architects: **Tom Green, Nigel V. Brown**

Date: 1997
Address: Bububu, 4 miles to the North of Stone Town, Zanzibar, Tanzania
More info tel.: +39 051 23 49 74 Fax: +39 01 23 90 86
www.salomes-garden.com
Photos: © Manolo Yllera

Style: rustic
Rooms: 4
Special features: large, unique rooms full of character. Private bathrooms, terrace, kitchen, central atrium and garden

TIGMI
A Place of Quietude to Listen to Silence

Architect: **Max Lawrence**

Address: Douar Tagadert el Kadi, Km 24 Route d'Amizmiz, Marrakech, Morocco
Tel.: +44 845 026 45 88
www.tigmi.com
Photos: © Pere Planells

Style: rustic
Rooms: 8
Special features: gardens, pool, terraces with 360º views, available on an exclusive basis for celebrating special occasions

DINAROBIN HOTEL

Golf & Spa, the Perfect Setting for Luxury Holidays in Mauritius

Architect: **Maurice Giraud**

Address: Le Morne Peninsula, Mauritius
Tel.: +11 230 401 49 00 Fax: +11 230 401 49 01
www.dinarobin-hotel.com
Photos: © Manolo Yllera

Style: tropical luxury
Rooms: 172 suites
Special features: golf course, land and sea sports, local band every night, miniclub, baby-sitter, boutiques, duty-free jewels, excursions, car hire, business center, conference facilities available

CHAPWANI PRIVATE ISLAND

Discover the Real Magic of Zanzibar

Architects: **Maura Antonietto, Nigel V. Brown**

Address: Chapwani Island, Zanzibar, Tanzania
More info tel.: +39 051 23 49 74 Fax: +39 01 23 90 86
www.chapwaniisland.com
Photos: © Manolo Yllera

Style: rustic
Rooms: 10
Special features: Oriental, African and European cuisine restaurant, boat transfers, excursion organization, diving

RIAD ZINA MARRAKECH
Your Hotel in Morocco

Architect: **Max Lawrence**

Address: Douar Tagadert el Kadi, Km 24 Route d'Amizmiz, Marrakech, Morocco
Tel.: +44 845 026 45 88
www.tigmi.com
Photos: © Pere Planells

Style: rustic
Rooms: 8
Special features: gardens, pool, terraces with 360° views, available on an exclusive basis
for celebrating special occasions

LAKE MANYARA TREE LODGE

Luxury Safari Lodges on the Northern Tanzanian Safari Circuit

Architect: **Chris Browne**

Address: Lake Manyara National Park, Northern Tanzania
Tel.: +27 11 809 4300
www.lakemanyara.com
Photos: © CC Africa

Style: rustic luxury
Rooms: 10 treehouse suites
Special features: en suite bathroom and outdoor shower, private game viewing deck overlooking the forest, crafts gallery and swimming pool, tours and safaris

DAR KAWA
Bed and Breakfast in Morocco

Architect: **Quentin Vilboux**

Address: 18 Derb EjWalie Kaat Benahid, Marrakech, Morocco
Tel.: +212 24 42 80 79
Photos: © Manolo Yllera

Style: traditional
Rooms: 4
Special features: typical *riad* from the XVII century in the center of Marrakech

BATELEUR CAMP
Luxurious Tented Safari Accommodation

Architect: **Chris Browne**

Address: Kichwa Tembo, Masai Mara National Reserve, Kenya
Tel.: +27 11 809 43 14
www.ccafrica.com/accommodation-1-id-2-11/lodgeid-2-1
Photos: © CC Africa

Style: rustic luxury
Rooms: 32
Special features: expansive en suite bathrooms, fans, private butler service, elegant
guest areas, lap pool, exciting safari activities

GRUMETI RIVER CAMP

Safari Accommodation at Grumeti

Architect: **Sylvio Rech**

Address: Western Serengeti, Tanzania
Tel.: +27 11 809 43 14
www.grumeti.com
Photos: © Manolo Yllera

Style: rustic
Rooms: tented suite
Special features: en suite bathrooms that offer separate WCs and alfresco showers
which open to the sun and stars, safaris

NOSSA SENHORA DA ASUNÇÃO POSADA

Perfect Harmony between Traditional and Modern Portugal

Architect: **José Paolo Santos**

Date: 1997
Address: Apartado 61, 7040 909 Arraiolos, Portugal
Tel.: +351 26 641 93 40 Fax: +351 26 641 92 80
www.portugalvirtual.pt/pousadas/arraiolos
Photos: © Pep Escoda

Style: traditional
Rooms: 2 intimate camps, each with 9 tented suites
Special features: restaurant, swimming pool, bar, air conditioning, tennis court,
meeting room, horse riding

RIAD DAR AMANE

Ideally Situated in the Center of Marrakech

Architect: Quentin Vilboux

Address: 33 Derb Mly Abdel Kader Derb Dabachi, 40000 Marrakech, Morocco
Photos: © Manolo Yllera

Style: rustic
Rooms: 4
Special features: safety deposit box, meeting/banquet facilities, baby-sitting, child services, solarium, internet services, fax/photocopying

CASAL DA DAMA
Tourism in the Country

Architects: **Unknown**

Date: 1998
Address: Rua Tenente José Henrique 10, Toxofal de Cima, 2530 Lourinhã, Portugal
Tel.: +351 261 41 10 53 Fax: +351 261 42 32 00
www.maisturismo.pt
Photos: © Pep Escoda

Style: traditional
Rooms: 1 double and 3 singles
Special features: bar, snack bar, golf course (10 km), swimming pool, parking,
tennis court

NGORONGORO CRATER LODGE
Sumptuous Safari Suites

Architects: **Silvio Rech & Lesley Carstens**

Address: Ngorongoro Crater, Serengeti National Park, Tanzania
Tel.: +27 11 809 43 14
www.ngorongorocrater.com
Photos: © CC Africa

Style: rustic luxury
Rooms: 3 intimate camps (2 with 12 suites, 1 with 6 suites)
Special features: fireplaces, exclusive butler service, safari shop, daily safaris to the Crater, birdwatching

QUINTA DO JUNCAL
Manor Guest House

Architect: **Manuel Morgado**
Interior designer: **Ana Isabel Domingo**

Date: 1980, recently restored
Address: 2525 Serra D'el Rei, Peniche, Portugal
Tel.: +351 262 90 50 30 Fax: +351 262 90 53 01
www.quintadojuncal.com
Photos: © Pep Escoda

Style: traditional
Rooms: 8 rooms and 3 cabins
Special features: gift shop, swimming pool, tennis court, driving range, hiking, historical, cultural and gastronomic circuits

POSADA LA BONITA

An Unspoiled Eden in Deep, Luxurious Jungle

Interior designer: **Franco Martini**

Date: 1999
Address: Paraje el Soberbio, Misiones, Argentina
Tel.: +54 3755 68 03 80
www.posadalabonita.com.ar
Photos: © Virginia del Giudice

Style: rustic
Rooms: 3 jungle huts
Special features: horse riding, kayaking, canoeing, excursions to waterfalls

QUINTA DO CAMPO

Tourism in a Manor House

Architect: **Teresa Nunes da Ponte (reconstruction)**

Date: 1994
Address: Rua Carles O'Neill 20, 2450-801 Valado dos Frades, Portugal
Tel.: +351 262 57 71 35 Fax: +351 262 57 75 55
www.quintadocampo.com
Photos: © Pep Escoda

Style: traditional
Rooms: 8 doubles and 7 suites
Special features: restaurant, self-service bar, cable TV, laundry, library, indoor games, gardens and pedestrian circuits, wedding and baptism celebrations

140

LA SARACINA

The Country Home, Born from a Thought of Love and a Dream of Beauty

Architects: **Unknown**

Date: 1991
Address: S.S. 146 Km 29,7, 53026 Pienza, Siena, Italy
Tel.: +39 0578 74 80 22 Fax: +39 0578 74 80 18
www.lasaracina.it
Photos: © Pep Escoda

Style: traditional
Rooms: 3 suites, 2 doubles, 1 apartment
Special features: swimming pool, tennis court, jacuzzi, garden

TENUTA SAN VITO

From the Land of Tuscany, the Warm Embrace of Beauty, Heart and Reason

Architects: **Unknown**

Date: 1985
Address: Via San Vito 59, 50056 Montelupo Florentino, Florence, Italy
Tel.: +39 0571 514 11 Fax: +39 0571 514 05
www.san-vito.com
Photos: © Pep Escoda

Style: traditional
Rooms: 4 apartments/villas
Special features: meeting lounge, swimming pool, weekly wine-tasting, mountain bikes

HOSPEDERÍA CONVENTO LA PARRA

Creating a Pleasant Time for Our Guests

Architect: **Francisco Viñao D'Lom (restoration)**
Interior designers: **María Ulecia & Javier Muñoz**

Date: 2000
Address: Santa María 16, La Parra, 06176 Badajoz, Spain
Tel.: +34 924 68 26 92 Fax: +34 924 68 26 19
www.laparra.net
Photos: © Pep Escoda

Style: traditional
Rooms: 21
Special features: gift shop, outdoor activities, cooking classes, convention room,
swimming pool

HOTEL TIVOLI PALACIO DE SETEAIS

Stunning Scenery and a Spectacular Setting

Architects: **Unknown**

Date: 1996
Address: Rua Barbosa du Bocage 10, Sintra 2710-517, Lisbon, Portugal
Tel.: +351 21 923 32 00 Fax: +351 21 923 42 77
www.tivolihotels.com
Photos: © Pep Escoda

Style: luxurious
Rooms: 30
Special features: restaurant, bar, laundry service, safe, baby-sitting, swimming pool, parking

TORRE DI BELLOSGUARDO

Hospitality and a Unique Atmosphere

Owner: **Amerigo Franchetti**

Interior designer: **Amerigo Franchetti**

Date: 1996
Address: Via Roti Michelozzi 2, 50124 Florence, Italy
Tel.: +39 055 229 81 45 Fax: +39 055 22 90 08
www.torrebellosguardo.com
Photos: © Pep Escoda

Style: traditional
Rooms: 8 doubles, 7 suites, 1 single
Special features: cooking classes, sports center, sauna, massage, flower garden, vegetable garden, vineyard, olive groves

PIRÁ LODGE

In Search of Gold

Architect: **Pablo Sánchez Elia**
Interior designer: **Laura Orcoyen**

Date: 2000
Address: Pasaje de El Boquerón, Mercedes, Corrientes, Argentina
Tel.: +54 1143 31 97 10 Fax: +54 3773 42 03 99
www.piralodge.com
Photos: © Virginia del Giudice

Style: rustic
Rooms: 5 doubles
Special features: kayaking, fly fishing, horse riding

TENUTA LE VISTE

Florence: Charming Luxury Hotel

Interior designer: **Rodolfo Bartoli**

Date: 1996
Address: Via del Leone 11, 50028 Mosciano, Florence, Italy
Tel.: +39 055 76 85 43 Fax: +39 055 76 82 19
www.tenuta-leviste.it
Photos: © Pep Escoda

Style: luxurious
Rooms: 4 doubles
Special features: satellite TV, huge park with olive trees and swimming pool,
own oil production

RESERVA ROTANA

Feel at Home in a Charming 17th Century Mansion

Architect: **Francisco Viñao D'Lom (restoration)**
Interior designers: **María Ulecia & Javier Muñoz**

Date: 1996
Address: Camí de S'Avall, Km 3, 07500 Manacor, Majorca, Spain
Tel.: +34 971 84 56 85 Fax: +34 971 55 52 58
www.reservarotana.com
Photos: © Pep Escoda

Style: traditional
Rooms: 22
Special features: minibar, satellite TV, air conditioning, heating, wine cellar, golf course

CA'S XORC

Enjoy Complete Well-being in an Incomparable
Environment

Architects: **Wolfgang Nikolaus Schmidt,
Juan Puigserver, Mariano Barceló**

Date: 2000
Address: Carretera de Deià, Km 56,1, 07100 Soller, Majorca, Spain
Tel.: +34 971 63 82 80 Fax: +34 971 63 29 49
www.casxorc.com
Photos: © Pep Escoda

Style: rustic
Rooms: 10 doubles
Special features: swimming pools, gardens, convention room with audiovisual
equipment, jacuzzi, sauna and steam bath

CATACURIAN

Gourmet Food & Wine Boutique Hotel

Architects: **Unknown**

Address: Progrès 2, 43736 El Masroig, Tarragona, Spain
Tel.: +34 977 82 53 41 Fax: +34 977 27 05 61
www.catacurian.net
Photos: © Pep Escoda

Style: traditional
Rooms: 18
Special features: restaurant and bar, cooking classes, visits to local wineries

EL ANTIGUO CONVENTO DE BOADILLA DEL MONTE

Cozy Atmosphere Surrounded by Magnificent Countryside

Architect: **José Ramón Duralde**

Address: Calle de las Monjas s/n, 28660 Boadilla del Monte, Madrid, Spain
Tel.: +34 916 32 22 20 Fax: +34 916 33 15 12
www.elconvento.net
Photos: © Pep Escoda

Style: traditional
Rooms: 18
Special features: restaurant, music and DJ services, wine tasting courses

BAIA BENIAMIN

Everything to Satisfy the Customers' Wishes

Interior designer: M. Carlo Brunelli

Date: 1986
Address: Corso Europa 63, Grimaldi Inferiore, Ventimiglia, Italy
Tel.: +39 0184 380 02 Fax: +39 0184 380 27
www.baiabeniamin.it
Photos: © Pep Escoda

Style: traditional luxury
Rooms: 5 doubles
Special features: safe, minibar, restaurant, bar, breakfast on the terrace overlooking
the bay, wine cellar, private beach, garden

LA LOCANDA DEL LOGGIATO
Medieval Village in Val d'Orcia

Owner: **Sabrina Marini**
Architect: **Sabrina Marini**
Interior designer: **Sabrina Marini**

Date: 2000
Address: Piazza del Moretto 30, Bagno Vignoni, Siena, Italy
Tel.: +39 0577 88 89 25
www.loggiato.it
Photos: © Pep Escoda

Style: rustic
Rooms: 6 doubles
Special features: each room has its own atmosphere, wine bar, wine cellar, thermal water pools

VILLA FONTELUNGA

Home Away from Home

Interior designer: **Philip Robinson**

Date: 2000
Address: Via Cunicchio 5, 52045 Arezzo, Tuscany, Italy
Tel.: +39 0575 66 04 10 Fax: +39 0575 66 19 63
www.fontelunga.com
Photos: © Pep Escoda

Style: rustic luxury
Rooms: 8 doubles, 1 twin
Special features: continental breakfast, air conditioning, laundry, modern en suite
showers and bathrooms, swimming pool

HOTEL VILLA FIESOLE

A Luxury Hotel in Tuscany

Architect: **Bianchini**

Interior designer: **Bianchini**

Date: 1995
Address: Via Beato Angelico 35, 50014 Florence, Italy
Tel.: +39 055 59 72 52 Fax: +39 055 59 91 33
www.villafiesole.it
Photos: © Pep Escoda

Style: luxurious
Rooms: 28 doubles
Special features: restaurant, bar, internet, laundry, massages, wedding celebrations